THE UNIVERSITY
WINC

DANTE'S EPIC JOURNEYS

Dante's
Epic
Journeys

David Thompson

The Johns Hopkins University Press
Baltimore and London

The Johns Hopkins University Press, Baltimore, Maryland 21218
The Johns Hopkins University Press Ltd., London

Library of Congress Catalog Card Number: 73-8112
ISBN 0-8018-1518-5

Library of Congress Cataloging in Publication data will be found on the last
printed page of this book.

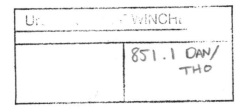

MAGISTRIS LUDI

J.H.
R.M.D.
J.F.

Contents

Preface

This essay in comparative literature represents the first extended attempt to relate Dante's major allegorical mode to classical and medieval interpretations of epic poetry rather than to patristic Biblical exegesis and also the first comprehensive explanation of Dante's enigmatic Ulysses. As such it constitutes, in a sense, the logical outcome of my principal studies and interests, particularly my interest in the classical tradition. However, I have been less concerned with tracing sources than with showing some ways in which one great writer made creative use of a rich and complex heritage. I hope to have thrown new light not only upon Dante's allegory—and thus upon the whole troubled question of exactly what an allegory was thought to be—but also upon the intricate relationship between poet and poem and between Dante's spiritual journeys and his written representation of those itineraries.

Appropriately enough, it was in Ithaca that I first
made Virgil's and Dante's acquaintance. The several portions of my study have since been written at diverse ports
of call; and along the way, grants (sometimes, be it ad-
mitted, ostensibly for different purposes) from the University of California, Los Angeles, the University of New
Mexico, and the University of Washington have facilitated
my research and writing, as have materials kindly supplied
by friends and colleagues on both coasts. My primary
debts, however, are acknowledged in the dedication.

Seattle, Washington

Acknowledgments

Portions of this essay, here more or less considerably expanded or revised, were published in *Dante Studies*, 85 (1967): 33–58 and *Viator*, 1 (1970): 201–6, the editors of which I thank for permission to reuse that material. I am also grateful to the Clarendon Press for allowing me to quote at length from an old favorite of mine, *Le opere di Dante Alighieri*, ed. E. Moore and P. Toynbee, 4th ed. (Oxford: Oxford University Press, 1924).

Introduction

In a *Comento* to some of his own sonnets, Lorenzo de'
Medici offers an explanation that may seem curious both to
readers of the ancient epic and to readers of the *Commedia*. To arrive at perfection, Lorenzo says, one must
first die with regard to lesser things. "It seems," he con-
tinues, "that this same opinion was held by Homer, Virgil,
and Dante: Homer sends Ulysses to the lower regions, Virgil sends Aeneas, and Dante sends himself to survey Hell,
in order to show that one goes to perfection by these ways
(*vie*). But after the cognition of imperfect things, it is
necessary to die with regard to them since, after Aeneas
reached the Elysian Fields and Dante had been led to Paradise, they remembered Hell no more."[1]

Why, one wonders, does Lorenzo so confidently regard the three poems as comparable in this fashion? To be

[1] Lorenzo de' Medici, *Scritti Scelti*, ed. Emilio Bigi, 2nd ed. (Torino:
UTET, 1965), pp. 314–15.

1

sure, Dante is often read along with Homer and Virgil in courses on "The Epic"; but as Ernst Curtius sternly remarked, "If [the *Commedia*] is commonly classed as 'epic,' that can be ascribed only to the inanity which thinks that the *Iliad* and *The Forsyte Saga* are to be spoken of in the same breath."[2]

If anything, we have become increasingly conscious of how Virgil differs from Homer, and Dante from just about every one. Indeed, modern scholarly discussions of the *Commedia* have tended to take place in a sort of literary vacuum: the *poema sacro* is deemed a unique work, comparable not to other poetic fictions but only to writings of a theological cast. Dante is God's scribe; his poem embodies a distinctively scriptural mode of figure or allegory; and our *accessus* to it must be via a study of the Bible and of patristic exegesis.

Such approaches have had considerable heuristic usefulness; they may even be said to have revolutionized our understanding of the *Commedia*. However, Dante's was not the first *poema sacro*: Macrobius (*Saturnalia* 1. 24. 13) had used just these words of the *Aeneid*, the author of which Dante calls his *maestro* and his *autore*.[3] As an authority, Virgil too had his exegetes; and although the *Commedia* is in most respects decidedly un-Virgilian,[4] it resembles the allegorized *Aeneid* in ways that tell us some-

---

[2] Ernst Robert Curtius, *European Literature and the Latin Middle Ages*, trans. Willard R. Trask, Bollingen Series, no. 36 (New York: Pantheon, 1953), pp. 361–62.

[3] Dante, *Inferno* 1. 85. On Dante's attitude toward Virgil and the *Aeneid*, see Robert Hollander, "Dante's Use of *Aeneid* I in *Inferno* I and II," *Comparative Literature*, 20 (1968): 142–56 (esp., 144–45).

[4] See J. H. Whitfield, *Dante and Virgil* (Oxford: Blackwell, 1949).

thing significant about where Dante stands in the European literary tradition.

Some years ago Theodore Silverstein studied Dante's "indebtedness to the *Aeneid* as it was transformed by both the allegorical commentaries and the mythographers." He gave special attention to a commentary by the twelfth-century Platonist, Bernard Silvestris; and having shown how Bernard transformed Aeneas's descent into "an ascent to the divine," Silverstein concluded that "Dante evidently conned [Vergil's] volume even better than we have hitherto observed. Among the number of those who describe the experience of the soul rising through the spheres to its Creator, among Augustine and Macrobius and Thomas Aquinas, among St Bernard and Hugh of St Victor and all the other mystics whom Dante knew, we must not fail to include Vergil the mystic, that Vergil who was Dante's master."[5]

The present essay is an attempt to explore the implications of Silverstein's insight. The search will perforce take us back to some of the earliest literary-philosophical discussions. Just as Homer's work lies behind Virgil's, so behind allegorizations of Virgil there lies a long history of Homeric interpretation, which ultimately also provides part of the context in which we should view Dante's enigmatic depiction of Ulysses. Although the *Commedia* is not an epic, Dante's journey—or as we shall see, journeys—will prove epic, in that they are comparable to those undertaken by the allegorists' Ulysses and Aeneas.

[5]H. Theodore Silverstein, "Dante and Vergil the Mystic," *Harvard Studies and Notes in Philology and Literature*, 14 (1932): 51–82.

part one

Three
Allegorical
Journeys

I

Dante's Twofold Itinerary

Are we to believe that in the thirty-fifth year of his life Dante Alighieri clambered down through a large hole in the earth, emerged on the other side, climbed a mountain, and finally ascended to the Empyrean? On the face of it, yes; for instead of relating a dream vision (like Scipio's, for example), the *Commedia* records a physical journey to God by a man in this life and in full possession of his senses. Yet we all know that such a journey is impossible; so the poem would seem to demand of us a virtually impossible suspension of disbelief.

To some readers the *Commedia* may present no such stumbling block; after all, they will ask, is it not a fiction? And in a fiction, of course, almost anything goes. If no one complains that Astolfo's journey to the moon was impossible, why worry about Dante's heavenly flight? A poet is no mere historian, fettered by brute fact.

But what if a poet claims to tell the truth?—if, instead of avowedly weaving a fable, he ventures to speak in a prophetic vein, on the basis of his own experience? How can the patently impossible make any claim to be true?

Perhaps we can best appreciate the peculiar nature of Dante's journey by comparing his account with that of another noted mountain climber. In a famous letter to Dionigi da Borgo San Sepolcro, Petrarch describes his ascent of Mount Ventoux, which he ostensibly climbed because it was there.[1] Although some portions of the narrative may seem straightforward enough, it soon becomes apparent that Petrarch's bodily progress (or lack of it) is an analogue of his inner life: the physical journey occasions a consideration of the spiritual. Lest this escape our attention, Petrarch sits down at one point and addresses himself in the following fashion:

Quod totiens hodie in ascensu montis huius expertus es, id scito et tibi accidere et multis, accedentibus ad beatam vitam; sed idcirco tam facile ab hominibus non perpendi, quod corporis motus in aperto sunt, animorum vero invisibiles et occulti.[2]

["What thou hast repeatedly experienced today in the ascent of this mountain, happens to thee, as to many, in the ascent toward the

---

[1] *Epistolae familiares* 4. 1. For a judicious discussion of the problems posed by this letter, see now Hans Baron, "Petrarch: His inner struggles and the humanistic discovery of man's nature," in *Florilegium Historiale, Essays Presented to Wallace K. Ferguson* (Toronto: University of Toronto Press, 1971), pp. 19–51 (esp., pp. 21–26).

[2] Francesco Petrarca, *Prose*, ed. G. Martellotti *et al.* (Milan: Ricciardi, 1955), pp. 834–36. The translation by James Harvey Robinson is reprinted in *Petrarch, A Humanist Among Princes*, ed. David Thompson (New York: Harper & Row, 1971), p. 30.

blessed life. But this is not so readily perceived by men, since the motions of the body are obvious and external while those of the soul are invisible and hidden."]

It has been the signal merit of Charles Singleton's work to demonstrate that the *Commedia* represents a two-fold itinerary: Dante's "obvious and external" journey is an analogue of the "invisible and hidden" spiritual course he followed, the *itinerarium mentis ad Deum*.[3] John Freccero, going a step further, has observed that since "pure experience is not directly communicable, being by definition unique," the whole poem is "an extended *exemplum* of *esperienza piena*," and that "it is in the experience that we must believe, not in the *exemplum*, the poem itself, which is his compromise, his expression of what for us is out of reach."[4]

Of course, Dante nowhere spells this out for us the way Petrarch does; but much in the poem that was formerly inexplicable makes sense once we realize that Dante is describing an *itinerarium mentis*.[5] For example, at the outset Dante's "firm foot was always the lower" (*Inf.* 1. 30: "il piè fermo sempre era il più basso") not because of how men climb actual mountains, but because one foot of his soul was lame and in need of cure. From moving by the

[3] See Charles S. Singleton, *Dante Studies 1. Commedia: Elements of Structure* (Cambridge, Mass.: Harvard University Press, 1957) and *Dante Studies 2. Journey to Beatrice* (Cambridge, Mass.: Harvard University Press, 1958).

[4] *Dante: A Collection of Critical Essays*, ed. John Freccero (Englewood Cliffs, New Jersey: Prentice Hall, 1965), pp. 2–3.

[5] See especially John Freccero, "Dante's Firm Foot and the Journey Without a Guide," *Harvard Theological Review*, 52 (1959): 245–81; and "Dante's Pilgrim in a Gyre," *PMLA*, 76 (1961): 168–81. On the wings of the

feet of the soul, Dante advances gradually to flying on the wings afforded him by Beatrice. Asked to cite the poem's main conceptual image, one might well choose the following (*Purg.* 12. 121–29):

> O superbi Cristian miseri lassi,
>> che, della vista della mente infermi,
>> fidanza avete ne' ritrosi passi;
> non v'accorgete voi, che noi siam vermi
>> nati a formar l'angelica farfalla,
>> che vola alla giustizia senza schermi?
> Di che l'animo vostro in alto galla,
>> poi siete quasi entomata in difetto,
>> sì come vermo, in cui formazion falla?

> [O proud Christians, wretched and weary,
>> who, sick in your mind's vision,
>> have faith in backward steps,
> do you not realize that we are worms
>> born to form the angelic butterfly,
>> which flies to judgment without defence?
> Why does your spirit soar on high
>> since you are, as it were, defective insects,
>> like a worm in which development is lacking?] *

---

soul, see Adhémar d'Alès, "Les ailes de l'âme," *Ephemerides Theologicae Louvanienses*, 10 (1933): 63–72. In his *Platonic Theology* (14.3), Ficino gives an excellent summation of the whole concept: "To conclude, our soul by means of the intellect and will, as by those twin Platonic wings, flies toward God, since by means of them it flies toward all things. By means of the intellect it attaches all things to itself; by means of the will, it attaches itself to all things. Thus the soul desires, endeavors, and begins to become God, and makes progress every day". I quote from the translation by Josephine Burroughs in *Journal of the History of Ideas*, 5 (1944): 238.

*My translation.

If this spiritual dimension of the poem was not immediately apparent, if indeed many fine critics have denied that the poem is allegorical, it has been largely because Dante's literal level is so fully realized, because "The particular, the individual, the concrete, the fleshed, the incarnate, is everywhere with the strength of reality and the irreducibility of reality itself."[6] Except in certain notable instances, Dante's language is representational, not referential; opaque, not transparent.

This distinction between the *Commedia* and other literary allegory (as he conceives of it) has led Professor Singleton to argue that Dante's poem must therefore have been written in imitation of scriptural allegory as it was interpreted in the Middle Ages.[7] It will be the argument of this chapter that Dante instead wrote allegory in the epic tradition, as it was conceived of in antiquity, in the Middle Ages, and in the Renaissance; and more specifically, that the *Aeneid*, as allegorized by Bernard Silvestris, afforded Dante a significant precedent for his twofold physical/spiritual journey.

[6] Singleton, *Commedia: Elements*, p. 13.

[7] For a critical assessment of the theories of Charles Singleton and Erich Auerbach, see my "Figure and Allegory in the *Commedia*," *Dante Studies*, 90 (1972): 1–11.

II

Odysseus among the Allegorists

Homer's Odysseus was a comparatively complicated man, realistic, resourceful, possessed of a strong intellectual curiosity—in many ways, an "untypical hero."[1] But in contrast to our notion of The Wanderer, the hero of the *Odyssey* had a very simple desire: to return home. To be sure, his curiosity does impel him to hear the sirens' song, and he does indeed seem rather to dally along the way; but the goal of his journey is Ithaca, and from the opening council of the gods we know that he will reach that goal. Even Nausicaa and the Phaeacian Utopia cannot stay his return to Penelope.

Odysseus, being more adaptable than his rather stolid peers, is seized upon by later writers for many purposes: his "complex personality becomes broken up into various

[1] W. B. Stanford, *The Ulysses Theme*, 2nd ed. (Oxford: Blackwell, 1963), chapter 5.

simple types—the *politique*, the romantic amorist, the sophisticated villain, the sensualist, the philosophic travel-ler, and others."[2] His detractors generally concentrated upon Odysseus's Trojan exploits. He naturally comes off rather badly in the *Aeneid*; and that text, along with Statius's *Achilleid*, afforded Dante an account of the sins for which Ulysses (with Diomedes) will be punished among the false counsellors (*Inf.* 26. 58–63):

> E dentro dalla lor fiamma si geme
>> l'aguato del caval che fe' la porta
>> ond' uscì de' Romani il gentil seme.
> Piangevisi entro l'arte per che morta
>> Deidamia ancor si duol d'Achille,
>> e del Palladio pena vi si porta.

> [And inside their flame they groan for
>> the ambush of the horse which made the gate-way
>> by which issued the noble seed of the Romans.
> They bewail within it the craft through which in death
>> Deidamia still grieves for Achilles,
>> and there they suffer punishment for the Pal-ladium.]

The Greek allegorists, on the other hand, present quite a different view of Odysseus.[3] Allegorical interpretation of Homer received part of its impetus from the attacks of philosophers who considered his picture of the gods a scan-dal. Plato's famous (or infamous) condemnation of the

---

[2] Ibid., p. 80.

[3] Much of the following account is drawn from Felix Buffière's exhaus-tive study, *Les mythes d'Homère et la pensée grecque* (Paris: Belles Lettres, 1956).

poet is merely the culmination of a long series of crit-
icisms. As early as the sixth century B.C., Xenophanes
had complained: "Both Homer and Hesiod have attributed
to the gods all things that are shameful and a reproach
among mankind: theft, adultery, and mutual deception."[4]
Granted, replied Homer's apologists—if we read him literally. But Homer's gods are actually personifications of natural forces, of the four elements, etc. Early Greek thinkers
were mostly natural philosophers, and allegorical interpretation found their various systems of thought already ex-
pressed in the Homeric poems: *Homeros physiologei.* Since
cosmogonical myths are largely absent from the *Odyssey*,
the allegorists concentrated upon the *Iliad*, whose divine
protagonists were easily identified with cosmic forces.

Later modes of allegorical interpretation are also a
good guide to the currents of philosophical thought. After
Socrates had given Greek philosophy a distinctly ethical
orientation, allegorists came to consider Homer not a natural scientist but a moralist: *Homeros paideuei.* Now the
Odyssey became the focus of their attention; and philosophers of various sects could agree that Odysseus represented the human ideal, the model of perfect wisdom. The
Cynics stressed his endurance, his indifference to hunger
and pain: he was their ideal ascetic. The Stoics had a similar view of him, although they tended to emphasize the
elements of labor and struggle in his life. Odysseus's adventures come to represent the wise man's battles against
many forms of vice and temptation: he struggles against
and overcomes the passions with the aid of gods (Hermes,

---

[4]Fragment 11, in Kathleen Freeman, *Ancilla to the Pre-Socratic Philosophers* (Cambridge, Mass.: Harvard University Press, 1957), p. 22.

Athena) who represent reason and wisdom. And as Socrates had rejected the study of the external world in order to focus on man, so Odysseus's leaving Calypso to return to Penelope depicts the renunciation of science for philosophy, the true wisdom.

This idea of Odysseus as the Sage, the perfect Wise Man triumphant over passion and adversity, finds expression in many Latin texts, perhaps nowhere more strikingly than in the conclusion to Apuleius's *De Deo Socratis*:

Nor does Homer teach you anything else [than what Accius does] with regard to the same Ulysses, in always representing Wisdom as his companion, whom he poetically calls Minerva. Hence, attended by her, he encounters all terrific dangers, and rises superior to all adverse circumstances. For, assisted by her, he entered the cavern of the Cyclops, but escaped from it; saw the oxen of the Sun, but abstained from them, and descended to the realms beneath, but emerged from them. With the same Wisdom for his companion, he passed by Scylla, and was not seized by her; he was surrounded by Charybdis, and was not retained by her; drank the cup of Circe, and was not transformed; he came to the Lotophagi, yet did not remain with them; he heard the Sirens, yet did not approach them.[5]

[5] *The Works of Apuleius* (London: Bell, 1902), p. 373. Cf. Horace, *Epistulae* 1.2. 17–18; Seneca, *De constantia sapientis* 2.2.1. That Ulysses represents *Sapientia* is a regular assumption of the mythographers, and the idea becomes a medieval commonplace: see *Scriptores rerum mythicarum latini tres*, G. H. Bode, ed. (reprinted., Hildesheim: Olms, 1968), 1:146. The philosophers' hero also becomes a Christian hero, even a figure of Christ: see Pierre Courcelle, "Quelques symboles funéraires du néo-platonisme latin," *Revue des études anciennes*, 46 (1944): 65–93 (esp., 90–91); and Hugo Rahner, "Odysseus at the Mast," *Greek Myths and Christian Mystery*, trans. Brian Battershaw (London: Burns & Oates, 1963), pp. 328–86. This highly favorable image of Ulysses persisted throughout the Middle Ages, most strikingly perhaps in the *Ovide Moralisé en prose* (*texte du quinzième siècle*), ed. C. de Boer (Amsterdam: North-Holland, 1954): "Nostre dit Sauveur Jhesucrist fu le sage orateur Ulixes" (p. 331).

Odysseus a Platonist's hero! The reconciliation of Homer
and Plato would seem almost complete; but Neoplatonists
carry the process still further, and Plotinus can even compare the catharsis of the soul with the journey of Odysseus:

'Let us flee then to the beloved Fatherland': this is the soundest
counsel. But what is this flight? How are we to gain the open sea?
For Odysseus is surely a parable to us when he commands the flight
from the sorceries of Circe or Calypso—not content to linger for all
the pleasure offered to his eyes and all the delight of sense filling his
days. The Fatherland to us is There whence we have come, and
There is The Father.[6]

The One, Intelligence, and the Soul "constitute the beloved native land to which Ulysses who is the wandering
soul in the sensible world is bound to return; and, like
Ulysses, the soul must flee from the enchantment of sensible things, from the charms of Circe."[7] This Odysseus is a
product of the third phase of ancient allegorical exegesis,
the mystical or theological (*Homeros theologei*).

While Stoicism and Epicureanism were being irrepara-
bly overthrown, the second century witnessed a revival of
Platonism in such figures as Apuleius and Numenius.
Platonism was taken up again partly because it satisfied
religious needs, just as did the mystery religions which
flourished at this time. These religions promised a rebirth
of the soul and this idea of renewal also figures large in the
Hermetic writings. Bréhier observes that "these transfor-
mations of the soul appear to us as mere changes of inter-

[6]Plotinus, *The Enneads*, trans. Stephen MacKenna, 2nd ed. (New York:
Pantheon, 1957), p. 63 (1. 6. 8).
[7]Emile Bréhier, *The Philosophy of Plotinus*, trans. Joseph Thomas
(Chicago: University of Chicago Press, 1958), p. 1.

nal states. But this could not be the case for the Hellenic imagination, which had a far too concrete conception of the soul not to imagine an inward transformation as a change of actual place, a passage from one place to another. The ascent or descent of the soul became a journey across the world."[8]

To the Neoplatonists, Homer was a truly inspired poet, not a mere imitator of imitations as Plato would have him. He drew his knowledge directly from the divine fount and dispensed it in a veiled and enigmatic form which only the initiated would understand. To Numenius, Odysseus's voyage was not just a series of adventures, or even a series of moral triumphs: rather, it represented the journey of the soul. The human soul descends from the heavens into the realm of generation and becoming, and is there a prisoner of the flesh; but eventually it regains its heavenly fatherland. Odysseus's long wanderings on the sea are an image of the soul's troubled exile in the world of matter; and the final trial imposed upon him by Tiresias—to travel until he should reach a people ignorant of the sea—signified the flight of the soul beyond this material realm.[9]

Thus, through a process of interpretation and reinterpretation, Odysseus's adventures became the great archetype for any journey or process, physical or spiritual; and whether they traverse the way of our life or the streets of Dublin, we will do well to view Odysseus's descendants through a Platonic glass.[10]

---

[8] Ibid. p. 35.

[9] On mystical interpretations of Ulysses in the Latin West, see Courcelle, "Quelques symboles funéraires du néo-platonisme latin," pp. 73–93.

[10] An important chapter in the *Fortleben* of this Neoplatonic Ulysses is discussed by W. B. Stanford, "The Mysticism That Pleased Him, a Note on the Primary Source of Joyce's *Ulysses*," *Envoy*, 5 (1951): 62–69.

III

Aeneas's
Spiritual
Itinerary

As we might expect, the Odyssean first part of the *Aeneid* has proven more susceptible of allegorical interpretation than have books 7 through 12, which describe what Aeneas does on completing his journey. Thus, in the twelfth century we find the great humanist John of Salisbury explaining:

Si verbis gentilium uti licet Christiano, qui solis electis diuinum et Deo placens per inhabitantem gratiam esse credit ingenium, etsi nec uerba nec sensus credam gentilium fugiendos, dummodo uitentur errores, hoc ipsum [i.e., the point John had made in the previous paragraph] diuina prudentia in Eneide sua sub inuolucro fictitii commenti innuisse visus est Maro, dum sex etatum gradus sex librorum distinctionibus prudenter expressit. Quibus conditionis humanae, dum Odisseam imitatur, ortum exprimere uisus est et processum, ipsumque, quem educit et prouehit et deducit ad Manes.[1]

[1] *Policraticus*, ed. Clemens Webb (Oxford, 1909), 2:415. The English version is from *Frivolities of Courtiers and Footprints of Philosophers*, trans. Joseph B. Pike (Minneapolis: University of Minnesota Press, 1938), p. 402.

[If the words of the pagan may be employed by the Christian who believes that a nature divine and pleasing to God because of the grace inherent in it can belong to the elect alone (although I do not think that either the words or the thoughts of the pagans are to be shunned provided their errors are avoided), Virgil seems to have been by divine wisdom given a hint of this very fact. Under the cloak of poetic imagination in his *Eneid* he subtly represents the six periods of life by the division of the work into six books. In these, in imitation of the *Odyssey*, he appears to have represented the origin and progress of man. The character he sets forth and develops he leads on and conducts down into the nether world.]

In this reading, books 1 through 6 take Aeneas from "the manifest tribulations of childhood, which is shaken by its own tempests," through "the varied errors of youth" (3) and "civic maturity" (5), to the sad end awaiting those not in a state of grace:

Since by now his emotions are numbed and his powers waning, he experiences not so much old age itself as its decay and, as it were, a descent to the lower world, to review there the errors of his past life, as though all his achievements had come to naught. He learns there that another way must be traveled by those who wish to attain the fond embraces of Lavinia and the destined kingdom of Italy as a sort of citadel of beatitude.[2]

John's brief allegorization is supposedly based on the commentary by his near-contemporary, Bernard Silvestris, who provided an extensive spiritual interpretation of the *Aeneid*.[3] However, whereas John uses the poem to point a

---

[2] *Frivolities*, p. 404.

[3] For an excellent survey of work on Bernard, see Giorgio Padoan, "Tradizione e fortuna del commento all' 'Eneide' di Bernardo Silvestre," *Italia medioevale e umanistica*, 3 (1960): 227–40, esp. note 4. To this can now be added J. Reginald O'Donnell, "The Sources and Meaning of Bernard Silvester's Commentary on the Aeneid," *Mediaeval Studies*, 24 (1962): 233–49; and Ter-

Christian moral, Bernard writes almost as though he were a late-antique Platonist, closer in spirit to Marius Victorinus than to Hugh of St. Victor.[4]

Bernard begins his *accessus* with a citation of Macrobius, to the effect that in the *Aeneid* Virgil provides philosophic truth in addition to the poetic fiction.[5] This being the case, a proper reading of the poem will be twofold, for one must consider Virgil as poet and Virgil as philosopher, in each case under three headings: subject (*unde agat, intentio*), method (*qualiter, modus agendi*) and purpose (*cur agat*).

In his capacity as poet, Bernard tells us, Virgil set out to unfold the misfortunes and toils of Aeneas and the other exiled Trojans. Since he wished to gain Augustus's favor, Virgil did not write according to the historical truth ("which Dares the Phrygian depicted"), but rather exalted Aeneas's deeds with fictions. Moreover, he wrote in imita-

---

rence Anthony McVeigh, "The Allegory of the Poets: A Study of Classical Tradition in Medieval Interpretation of Virgil" (Ph.D. dissertation, Fordham University, 1964; University Microfilms 64–8587), pp. 142–83. Professor J. W. Jones, Jr., of the College of William and Mary, is working on a new edition of Bernard's commentary, which will considerably improve the text used here, *Commentum Bernardi Silvestris super sex libros Eneidos Virgilii*, ed. Guilielmus Riedel (Greifswald, 1924), which I shall be citing by page and line number.

[4] On late-antique readings of Virgil, see Pierre Courcelle, "Les Pères de l'Église devant les Enfers Virgiliens," *Archives d'histoire doctrinale et littéraire du Moyen Age*, 22 (1955): 5–74; and "Interprétations néo-platonisantes du livre VI de l'*Énéide*," *Recherches sur la Tradition Platonicienne*, Fondation Hardt pour l'Étude de l'Antiquité Classique, Entretiens, 3 (Geneva: Vandoeuvres, 1955): 95–136.

[5] For much of the basic bibliography on the *accessus* form, one may consult Hubert Silvestre, "Le schéma 'moderne' des *accessus*," *Latomus*, 16 (1957): 684–89. Some of the technical problems posed by Bernard's very interesting *accessus* call for a separate study, which I hope to publish in the near future.

tion of Homer, so that *Aeneid* 2 corresponds to the *Iliad*, and the rest of the poem to the *Odyssey* (1.13–23).[6]

With regard to Virgil's method, Bernard observes that there are two narrative arrangements, the natural and the artificial. The natural is when things are narrated in the order in which they happened, as in the works of Lucan and Statius. An artificial arrangement has the poem begin in mid-story, then recur to the beginning; this is what Virgil did, for in books 2 and 3 Aeneas tells Dido about the fall of Troy and his subsequent wanderings (1.24–2.11).

As for the *cur agat*, Bernard explains that some poets write for the sake of usefulness (*causa utilitatis*), like the satirists; others for the sake of pleasure (*causa delectationis*), like the comic poets; and others for the sake of both, like the narrative poets (2.14–16).[7] The style of the *Aeneid* and the deeds described offer a certain pleasure. At the same time, the work has a twofold usefulness: imitation of its style will gain one great skill in writing, and the poem's content offers *exempla* that spur one to follow the honorable course and avoid the unlawful (2.19–27). For example: "ex laboribus Eneae tolerantiae exemplum habemus" (2.28: "from the toils of Aeneas we have a model of endurance"). The moral import of the *Aeneid*, then, is conveyed by the literal, poetic level, with no need for allegorization; and Bernard's estimate of Virgil the poet

---

[6] Like John, however, Bernard confines himself to the first six books of the *Aeneid*. Even Fulgentius, who had set out to read the poem as a progression from *natura* to *doctrina* to *felicitas*, had had very little to say about the last six books.

[7] Bernard quotes Horace, *Ars poetica*, 333–34: "aut prodesse volunt aut delectare poetae/ aut simul atque iocunda et idonea dicere vitae."

is very like what we will later find Dryden saying about the epic poem: "The design of it is to form the mind to heroic virtue by example; 'tis conveyed in verse, that it may delight while it instructs."[8]

Bernard's real interest lies not in Virgil the poet-moralist, however, but in Virgil the philosopher; and it is in the last part of the *accessus* that he lays the groundwork for his whole commentary on the *Aeneid*:

Scribit enim in quantum est philosophus humanae vitae naturam. Modus vero agendi talis est: sub integumento[9] describit quid agat vel quid patiatur humanus spiritus in humano corpore temporaliter positus. Atque in hoc scribendo naturali utitur ordine, atque ita utrumque narrationis ordinem observat, artificialem poeta, naturalem philosophus (3.11–17).

[Insofar as he is a philosopher, he writes about the nature of human life. This is his manner of treatment: under a covering he describes what the human spirit does or what it undergoes when placed for a time in the human body. And in writing about this he uses the natural order; and thus he observes both narrative arrangements, the artificial as poet, the natural as philosopher.] *

---

[8] *Of Dramatic Poesy and Other Critical Essays*, ed. George Watson (London: Dent, 1962) 2: 223–24.

[9] Bernard goes on to explain: "Integumentum vero est genus demonstrationis sub fabulosa narratione veritatis involvens intellectum, unde et involucrum dicitur" (3.18–20: "Integument is the type of demonstration wrapping the thing understood under a fabulous narration of the truth, wherefore it is also called *involucrum* [wrapper, envelope]"—as in the first passage quoted above from John of Salisbury). On the whole, *integumentum* seems to have been used in reading pagan authors (cf. John of Garland's *Integumenta Ovidii*), *allegoria* when reading the Bible: see Edouard Jeauneau, "L'usage de la notion d'*integumentum* à travers les gloses de Guillaume de Conches," *Archives d'histoire doctrinale et littéraire du Moyen Age*, 24 (1957): 35–100, esp. p. 37.

---

*My translation.

Finally, self-knowledge (*sui agnitionem*) can be obtained from this poem: "homini vero magna utilitas est, ut ait Macrobius, si se ipsum cognoverit" (3.21–22: "it is a great benefit to a man, as Macrobius says, if he knows himself").

Without thinking to distinguish between *ordo artificialis* and *ordo naturalis*, Fulgentius had read the *Aeneid* as an allegory depicting the ages of man. In his commentary, Bernard retains Fulgentius's basic scheme—much more closely, in fact, than John of Salisbury was to do—reading book 1 as a story of *infantia*, 2 as *pueritia*, and so on; but he also adds a new dimension. In his interpretation the poem becomes a Platonic allegory, the story of the human soul imprisoned in its mortal body.

The basic difference between Fulgentius's allegorization and Bernard's is well illustrated by a comparison of their interpretations of the storm and shipwreck with which the *Aeneid* opens. Fulgentius has Virgil explain:

Naufragium posuimus in modum periculosae natiuitatis, in qua et maternum est pariendi dispendium uel infantum nascendi periculum. In qua necessitate uniuersaliter humanum uoluitur genus. Nam ut euidentius hoc intellegas, a Iunone, quae dea partus est, hoc naufragium generatur. Nam et Eolum inmittit; Eolus enim Grece quasi eonolus, id est saeculi interitus. . . . [10]

[I introduced a shipwreck to represent the danger of birth in which there is a risk for the mother in giving birth and a danger for the infant in birth itself. The human race is universally involved in this necessity. And that you might understand this more clearly, this

---

[10]Fulgentius, *Opera*, ed. Rudolph Helm (Leipzig: Teubner, 1898), p. 91. The English version is from McVeigh, "The Allegory of the Poets," p. 209, who in an appendix (pp. 201–53) offers the first translation of the *Expositio Continentiae Virgilianae* along with an extensive commentary.

shipwreck was stirred up by Juno, who is the goddess of birth. She sends Eolus; in Greek Eolus is *eonolus*, that is, destruction of life.]

Why the goddess of birth should *send*, rather than forfend, "destruction of life" may be a bit difficult to understand in this purely physiological context, but in Bernard's Platonic reading Eolus's presence makes perfect sense:

Eolum vero legimus regem esse ventorum qui ventis mare commovit. Per hunc intelligimus nativitatem pueri qui dicitur Eolus quasi eon olus i. e. seculi interitus, quia nascente homine seculum i. e. vita animae interit, dum gravedine carnis oppressa a divinitate sua descendit et libidini carnis assentit (4.29–5.4).

[We read that Eolus is king of the winds, who stirs up the sea with winds. By him we understand the boy's birth, which is called Eolus—as it were, *eon olus*, that is, destruction of life—because at a man's birth *seculum*, that is the life of the soul, perishes, while overcome by the heaviness of the flesh it descends from its divinity and assents to the desire of the flesh.] [11] *

Whereas Fulgentius says nothing about the soul, Bernard glosses Aeneas as "ennos demas i. e. habitator corporis" (10.12: "*ennos demas*, that is, inhabitant of the body"), and interprets his adventures as the spirit's erring, but finally successful, journey to Italy "quae incrementum interpretatur naturam animi accipimus quae est rationalitas et immortalitas, virtus, scientia" (20.11–13: "which alle-

---

[11] For a further elaboration of this topic, see below, part 2, chapter 9. Platonic ideas about the descent of the soul could of course present Christian exegetes with a serious difficulty: see, for example (on William of Conches's glosses on Macrobius's commentary on Cicero's *Somnium Scipionis*), Edouard Jeauneau, "Macrobe, source du platonisme chartrain," *Studi Medievali*, 3rd series, 1 (1960): 3–24 (esp. pp. 16–20).

*My translation.

gorically interpreted we take as the nature of the soul, which is rationality and immortality, virtue, knowledge"). Of this spiritual *iter* Bernard says: "in hac vita itur ad contemplationem, in alia ad ora i. e. ad videndum facie ad faciem" (52.4–5: "in this life one journeys to contemplation, in the other *ad ora* [to the countenance], that is, to seeing face to face"). Here Bernard clearly echoes Paul's "Videmus nunc per speculum in aenigmate; tunc autem facie ad faciem" (I Corinthians 13:12: "For now we see through a glass darkly; but then face to face"). By assimilating the *Aeneid* to the whole Platonic-Christian tradition of spiritual progress, Bernard makes the poem an allegory structurally very like that of the *Commedia*, in which Dante's physical journey, the literal level of the poem, figures another journey—a spiritual itinerary that takes place *in hac vita*. Thus the allegorized epic afforded Dante a close paradigm for his major allegorical mode, and Virgil may have been Dante's *maestro* in a way we had not heretofore realized.[12]

---

[12] Perhaps one cannot prove conclusively that Dante knew Bernard's *Commentum*; for as Curtius observed, "He conceals his sources as he does his education and the story of his youthful years" (*European Literature*, p. 360). Padoan ("Tradizione e fortuna," pp. 227–40) has shown that the work was known in Italy, however, and it is to be hoped that he will follow up his intention to write at length on how "l'interpretazione medievale della Nekyia virgiliana (per la quale alcuni brevi accenni del Silvestre sono molto interessanti) ha influenzato in modo determinante la fantasia dell'autore della *Divina Commedia*, come bene intese il figlio suo, Pietro" (p. 240).

IV

Letter
and
Allegory

The *Odyssey*, the *Aeneid* and the *Commedia* all, then, can be regarded as physical journeys representing spiritual journeys to the soul's *patria*; and in this light, it is no wonder that Dante had himself welcomed into "la bella scuola/ di quel signor dell' altissimo canto" (*Inf.* 4. 94-95: "the splendid school/ of that master of loftiest song").[1]

The modern reader will very likely find Numenius and company dangerous guides through the world of Odysseus,[2] and Bernard Silvestris at best an interesting

[1] For Dante's spiritual interpretation of Lucan, see *Convivio* 4. 28, and also the acute remarks on that passage by Phillip Damon, *Modes of Analogy in Ancient and Medieval Verse*, University of California Publications in Classical Philology 15, no. 6 (1961): 331.

[2] See, however, Buffière, *Les Mythes d'Homère*, pp. 4-5; and Frederick Combellack (reviewing Buffière): "One cannot help being impressed as one reads some portions of this book by the similarity between much of the ancient allegorical interpretation of Homer and much modern literary criticism" (*Classical Philology*, 54 (1959): 136).

specimen of twelfth-century Platonist. But the validity of their allegorizations is not at issue here. What I wish to stress is that to any reader, of whatever persuasion, the *Odyssey* and the *Aeneid* are obviously mimetic: real human beings love and fight and shed blood and die. They may seem less vivid and realistic in their mimesis than the *Commedia* (at least, the infernal portion of Dante's poem), but this is a matter of convention and expectation. (Racine and Voltaire probably found Dido a good deal more "real" than Beatrice—as may we.) Nausicaa and Dido and Beatrice are all intended to have the same mimetic status as, say, Natasha or Grushenka—they are flesh and blood, not referential personifications.[3] Thus, making due allowances for their differences in style, we may say that both epic poems have the same sort of literal level as the *Commedia*, "given in the focus of single vision."[4] If they were also regarded as allegories, clearly for classical and medieval readers, a poetic allegory could show us "the concrete, the fleshed, the incarnate" with all the "irreducibility of reality itself." And if this seems strange to us, it is because we still permit ourselves to be victimized by Romantic prejudices about the nature of allegory.[5]

[3] We would all do well to take Lionel Friedman's advice to "divorce **ALLEGORY** from **PERSONIFICATION**, two entirely separate concepts which moderns—but not medieval man—insist on confusing" (*Romance Philology*, 20 [1966]: 124). Cf. the recent judicious little book by Jean Pépin, *Dante et la Tradition de l'Allégorie* (Inst. d'Etudes Médiévales: Montreal, 1970), p. 19. Medieval studies have been unduly influenced by C. S. Lewis; elsewhere there is a sounder view of allegory as significant action, e.g. in G. S. Kirk, *Myth, Its Meaning and Functions in Ancient and Other Cultures* (Los Angeles: University of California Press, 1971).

[4] Singleton, *Commedia: Elements*, p. 15.

[5] See David Thompson, "Allegory and Typology in the *Aeneid*," *Arethusa*, 3 (1970): 147–53.

But be that as it may, it probably is fair to say that for most of us the major interest of the *Commedia* lies in its literal level. We care more about the characters that Dante meets along the way than about the spiral psychic course that brings him there. In my view, the major problem now facing Dante criticism (if we can agree to a moratorium on worrying about *poesia* and *non poesia*, and "the allegory of poets" versus "the allegory of theologians") is to find a satisfactory relation between this literal level and the allegorical dimension of the poem. The second part of my essay aims to make a contribution in this direction.

part two

Ulysses,
Aeneas,
Dante

V

Ulysses and the Critics

Individual characters in the *Inferno* have often been viewed as projections of Dante's own personality; and, with the possible exception of Francesca, Ulysses has proved the most frequent object of such interpretations. Thus Benedetto Croce declared that "no one of his age was more deeply moved than Dante by the passion to know all that is knowable, and nowhere else has he given such noble expression to that noble passion as in the great figure of Ulysses."[1]

Bruno Nardi advanced a similar theory in an essay that set the terms for most subsequent discussions of Ulysses.[2] He noted that Dante, like Ulysses, had been

---

[1] Quoted by John D. Sinclair, *The Divine Comedy of Dante Alighieri*, Book 1: *Inferno* (New York: Oxford University Press, 1958), p. 331.

[2] Bruno Nardi, "La tragedia d'Ulisse," *Dante e la cultura medievale: Nuovi saggi di filosofia dantesca*, 2nd ed. (Bari: Laterza, 1949), pp. 153-65.

37

forced to wander from place to place. Also, he found in both Ulysses and Dante the belief that knowledge constitutes the ultimate basis of human happiness. Hence Ulysses, admirable but doomed, illustrates a profound conflict in the mind of the poet—a conflict between the theologian's condemnation and the emotion with which Ulysses' bold enterprise is evoked. "The brief words with which Ulysses inspires his ardor in his companions burst forth from Dante's deepest convictions. Ulysses leaps out, bold and undaunted, from the very heart of the poet, who sails on the tragic ship at the hero's side" (p. 163). And although Mario Fubini takes issue with Nardi on some points, he holds a similar opinion about the grandeur and nobility of Ulysses' quest, and about the relation between Dante and his creation: "Who does not hear the heart of Dante himself beating in Ulysses' *orazion picciola?*"[3]

But Rocco Montano will not accept this "confusion between Dante the poet and his damned creatures."[4] He grants that Dante had felt the fascination of pure intellectual inquiry, the temptation to a vain use of the intelligence. After all, a poet can hardly represent something of which he has had no experience at all; but the ability to represent something is not the same as actual participation in it. Far from being a spokesman for the author, "Ulysses is, in Dante's mind, the incarnation of a vain and distorted investigation, of a search for knowledge that for the poet, as for the whole medieval world, was *curiositas*, sin, *prosti-*

---

[3] Mario Fubini, "Il peccato di Ulisse," *Due studi danteschi* (Florence: Sansoni, 1951), p. 17.

[4] Rocco Montano, "Il 'folle volo' di Ulisse," *Suggerimenti per una lettura di Dante* (Naples: Conte Editore, 1956), pp. 131–66 (esp., p. 141); and in the same volume, "Una nota per Fubini," pp. 175–78.

tutio nostrae virtutis rationalis" (p. 175). In Montano's
view, readings of the Ulysses canto have been vitiated by a
false view of poetry, a faulty and outmoded aesthetics; and
at the heart of his critique lies a polemic against an anach-
ronistic "romantic sensibility."

Montano's trenchant critique scores off Nardi and
Fubini at many points, and we can be grateful to him for
drawing some distinctions that had been too easily over-
looked in the general rush to appropriate Ulysses and his
creator for the modern world. Whatever our reactions to
Ulysses' speech, it should be clear that the same author
creates both the heroes and the villains and is not neces-
sarily to be identified with either. Yet there is a further
distinction to be drawn. When Nardi and Montano refer to
a Dante who does or does not find expression in the figure
of Ulysses, they presumably refer to the Dante who writes
the poem, Dante *poeta*. But we have learned to distinguish
carefully between Dante the pilgrim and Dante the
poet, between the pilgrim who faints in sympathy at
the tale of Francesca and the poet who put her in Hell. In
the case of Dante, this is more than a literary distinction
between author and *persona*; for the Dante who writes the
poem is quite literally a different man from the one who
makes the journey described in it.[5] Conversion has made
Dante a new man; and from his new perspective he can
look back upon his old self, just as Augustine had reviewed
critically his preconversion existence. I hope to show that

[5]I do not mean to suggest that Montano ignores this distinction; indeed, he might almost claim to have discovered it. But the distinction opens
various perspectives upon the poem, and is in any case not a sure formula for
assessing every passage or episode. See the critique by Joseph Mazzeo, *Comparative Literature*, 9 (1957): 169.

there is no necessary contradiction between Montano's assertion that Dante does not portray himself in the figure of Ulysses and Nardi's feeling that Ulysses represents Dante in some significant respects. I suggest that in Ulysses Dante has rendered one aspect of his preconversion self, that we have (*ut ita dicam*) the portrait of the artist as a middle-aged man.

VI

*Ulysses
in the
Commedia*

Because book 6 of the *Aeneid* is Dante's most important literary precedent for his descent to the underworld, a brief comparison between Aeneas's experience and that of Dante will help to highlight certain significant features of the *Inferno*.

In his progress through Hades, Aeneas has a series of dramatic encounters with shades that are known to him personally. First, among the unburied, he comes upon his pilot, Palinurus, who had been swept overboard en route from Sicily. Next, in the Fields of Mourning, he has a tearful encounter with Dido. And then, among the famous warriors, he meets Deiphobus, who had perished in the fall of Troy. These three represent (in a reverse temporal order) Aeneas's past, a past that is dead; and only by re-encountering, by reexperiencing his past, could he leave it behind him: "Not until he had faced and left the unappeased guilt and empty nostalgia of his old self, could he be ready for the realities of his future."[1]

But Aeneas does not even see Tartarus, the closest classical equivalent to Hell; rather, he hears about it from the Sibyl. On the basis of Aeneas's encounters thus far, we might expect to find there a variety of nefarious individuals from the realm of his own experience—Paris, perhaps, or Clytemnestra. Instead, Virgil provides merely a standard array of infamous rebels against the authority of Jupiter: the Titans, Salmoneus, Tityos, Ixion—all impressive enough in their way, but unrelated to Aeneas's life. The classical epic hero has no intimate contact with the classical Hell.

We may contrast this with Dante's trip through the underworld. In enjoining him to write about what he has seen, Cacciaguida says (*Par.* 17. 127–42):

> Ma nondimen, rimossa ogni menzogna,
> tutta tua vision fa manifesta,
> e lascia pur grattar dov'è la rogna;
> chè se la voce tua sarà molesta
> nel primo gusto, vital nutrimento
> lascerà poi quando sarà digesta.
> Questo tuo grido farà come vento,
> che le più alte cime più percote;
> e ciò non fa d'onor poco argomento.
> Però ti son mostrate in queste rote,
> nel monte, e nella valle dolorosa,
> pur l'anime che son di fama note;

---

[1] Brooks Otis, *Virgil: A Study in Civilized Poetry* (Oxford: Clarendon Press, 1963), p. 297. Otis's analysis of the *Aeneid* has, I think, considerable relevance to the *Commedia.*

chè l'animo di quel ch'ode non posa,
    nè ferma fede per esemplo ch'haia
    la sua radice incognita e nascosa,
nè per altro argomento che non paia.

[But nonetheless, all falsehood put aside,
    show everything that you see,
    and let there be scratching where the itch is;
for if what you say is unpleasant
    at first taste, it will afterwards leave
    life-giving nourishment when it is digested.
This outcry of yours will be like the wind,
    which strikes the loftiest summits hardest;
    and that is no little proof of honor.
Therefore you have been shown—in these heavens,
    on the mountain, and in the woeful valley—
    only souls that are known to fame;
for the listener's mind does not pause
    or fix its faith through an example
    which has its origin unknown and hidden,
or through any other argument that is not apparent.] *

In Hell, Dante does see souls that we would naturally think of as "known to fame," the notorious sinners out of the past, both mythological (Capaneus, Jason) and historical (Pyrrhus, Brutus). Indeed, the juxtaposition of Dido, Cleopatra, and Helen (*Inf.* 5. 61–64) shows how continuous the mythological and historical realms were in Dante's imagination. But in keeping with the immediate, practical purpose of the poem, Dante also includes a different class of famous souls—those who would be familiar to his original audience and, in many cases, known to himself. The memorable figures of the *Inferno*, the figures to whom

*My translation.

Dante devotes separate cantos (and to whom De Sanctis and a host of others have devoted separate essays), spring not from the classical or legendary past, but from Dante's Italy. Francesca, Farinata, Pier delle Vigne, Brunetto Latini, Nicholas III, Guido da Montefeltro, Ugolino: friend or foe, they are sometimes comparable to Dido and Deiphobus, but they are a far cry from the remote inhabitants of Tartarus. Dante's own contemporaries (or near contemporaries), not an array of traditional cameo figures, play the lead characters in his infernal cast.

There is, however, one exception. Amidst these Italians from the Duecento, and yet so apparently appropriate that we tend to overlook the anomaly, stands the figure of Ulysses, whose account of his last voyage and shipwreck dominates the twenty-sixth canto and constitutes one of the acknowledged high points of the *Inferno*.

Dante did not have to ransack Greek mythology just to find an interesting sinner for the eighth *bolgia*: in the very next canto Guido da Montefeltro affords a striking modern example of an evil counsellor. Only for this bolgia, in fact, does Dante create two such elaborate depictions. He has gone far out of his usual way to include Ulysses' story. This alone would suggest that there is something especially important and problematic about Ulysses; and our initial impression is reinforced by Dante's recurrent preoccupation with him.

After emerging from Hell, and before beginning to climb the mountain, Dante and Virgil walked along the lonely plain. Virgil washed Dante's face, and then they came to a shore (*Purg.* 1. 130–33):

> Venimmo poi in sul lito diserto,
> che mai non vide navicar sue acque

uomo, che di tornar sia poscia esperto.
Quivi mi cinse sì come altrui piacque.

[We came then to the desert shore,
which never saw any one sail its waters
who was afterwards able to return.
There he girded me as it pleased another.] *

Topography and language alike summon to mind Ulysses'
ill-starred voyage. The rhyme itself recalls his narrative (cf.
esperto and *deserto* at *Inf.* 26. 98,102), and *come altrui
piacque* echoes the description of his shipwreck within
sight of this very mountain in the southern hemisphere
(*Inf.* 26. 130–42):

Cinque volte racceso, e tante casso
lo lume era di sotto dalla luna,
poi ch'entrati eravam nell'alto passo,
quando n'apparve una montagna bruna
per la distanza, e parvemi alta tanto
quanto veduta non n'aveva alcuna.
Noi ci allegrammo, e tosto tornò in pianto;
chè dalla nuova terra un turbo nacque,
e percosse del legno il primo canto.
Tre volte il fe' girar con tutte l'acque,
alla quarta levar la poppa in suso,
e la prora ire in giù, com'altrui piacque,
infin che il mar fu sopra noi richiuso.

[Five times the light beneath the moon
had been kindled, and as often quenched,
since we had entered on the arduous passage,
When there appeared to us a mountain dark
through the distance, and it seemed to me
higher than any I had ever seen.

*My translation.

We felt joy, and soon it turned to woe;
    for from the new land a whirlwind arose,
    and it struck the front part of our ship.
Three times it made it spin along with the waters,
    at the fourth it made the stern rise up,
    and the prow go down, as it pleased another,
until the sea closed over us.] *

Then, further along in Purgatory, we have an explicit reference to Ulysses. After viewing examples of zeal and sloth on the fourth terrace, Dante goes off on a wandering train of thought; his *pensamento* turns into a *sogno*; and in this dream there appears to him a *femmina balba* who sings bewitchingly (*Purg.* 19. 19–24):

"Io son," cantava, "io son dolce Sirena,
    che i marinari in mezzo mar dismago;
    tanto son di piacere a sentir piena.
Io volsi Ulisse del suo cammin vago
    al canto mio; e qual meco si ausa
    rado sen parte, sì tutto l'appago."

["I am," she sang, "I am the sweet Siren,
    who leads sailors astray in mid-sea;
    it is such a pleasure to hear me.
I turned Ulysses, intent upon his way,
    to my song; and whoever abides with me
    rarely leaves, so wholly do I gratify him."] *

A *donna santa* appears beside Dante and calls upon Virgil. He in turn tears open the siren's clothes and exposes her belly, and the stench awakens Dante from his dream.

*My translation.

48

Finally, when Dante is far aloft and about to ascend to the Primum Mobile, Beatrice tells him to look down and see how far he has turned. He looks—and the first thing that catches his attention is "di là da Gade il varco/folle d'Ulisse" (*Par.* 27. 82–83: "beyond Cadiz the mad course of Ulysses"). So Ulysses is not just another (albeit vividly portrayed) inhabitant of Hell. He figures in each of the three cantiche; and even before entering into an analysis of these appearances we can safely assert that Dante makes him a creature of more than temporary or incidental interest.

Ulysses' various appearances are notable enough, but even more immediately striking is the sort of thing that Dante tells us about him. Aside from the list of sins that landed Ulysses in Hell, and a few details of his story (e.g., his having stayed with Circe), Dante has invented the entire account of Ulysses, not only the final voyage but also the quoted version of his encounter with the siren. And he has invented these episodes not to fill gaps in the story as known to himself and his Greekless contemporaries, but in direct opposition to a perfectly clear tradition.

From Dares and Dictys, or from the extensive literary texts dependent upon them, Dante could easily have learned about Ulysses' return to Ithaca and how he died there. And these were not the only obvious sources of information. Classical texts cast considerable light upon Ulysses' fate, but if we consider these sources too vague, we need only turn to the various mythographers. Hyginus, for example, gives us the several stages of Ulysses' homeward voyage, step by step. After lying with Circe and siring Telegonus, Ulysses proceeds to Avernus for his *descensus ad inferos.* Then, warned by Circe, he passes successfully by the sirens, reaches home, destroys the suitors, and eventually dies at the hands of Telegonus.[2]

I think we can assume that if Dante was the least bit curious about Ulysses, he may be expected to have found his way to one or another of these sources. Without laboring the point unduly, I should like to suggest that Benvenuto da Imola was right when he asserted: "But whatever may be said, I cannot be persuaded to believe that Dante was ignorant of what even schoolboys know; so I say that rather the author devised this on purpose."[3] Dante was so interested in Ulysses that he first made a special point of including him, and then changed the accepted story in a radical fashion. But for what purpose? What had Ulysses to do with Dante, and Dante with Ulysses?

---

[2]*Auctores mythographi latini*, ed. A. van Staveren (Leyden, 1742), pp. 218 ff. See also *Scriptores rerum mythicarum latini tres*, ed. G. H. Bode (reprint ed., Hildesheim: Olms, 1968), 1: 5, 15, 56–57, 108–9.

[3]Quoted by Giorgio Padoan, "Ulisse 'fandi fictor' e le vie della sapienza," *Studi danteschi*, 37 (1960): 35, n. 1.

VII

Ulysses
and
Aeneas

Seneca had complained about people who wasted their time in vain speculations about Ulysses' route:

Do you raise the question, "Through what regions did Ulysses stray?" instead of trying to prevent ourselves from going astray at all times? We have no leisure to hear lectures on the question whether he was sea-tost between Italy and Sicily, or outside our known world (indeed, so long a wandering could not possibly have taken place within its narrow bounds); we ourselves encounter storms of the spirit, which toss us daily, and our depravity drives us into all the ills which troubled Ulysses. For us there is never lacking the beauty to tempt our eyes, or the enemy to assail us; on this side are savage monsters that delight in human blood, on that side the treacherous allurements of the ear, and yonder is shipwreck and all the varied category of misfortunes. Show me rather, by the example of Ulysses, how I am to love my country, my wife, my father, and how, even after suffering shipwreck, I am to sail toward these ends, honourable as they are.[1]

[1] *Epistulae morales* 88. 7, trans. Richard M. Gummere, Loeb Classical Library (Cambridge: Harvard University Press, 1953). Cf. Albin Lesky, *A*

53

Ulysses interests the Stoic as a useful example of a man, who, even in the face of difficulties, reached his domestic goal.

Dante has Ulysses' speech open on exactly the opposite note (*Inf.* 26. 90–99):

> Quando
> mi diparti' da Circe, che sotrasse
>   me più d'un anno là presso a Gaeta
>   prima che sì Enea la nominasse;
> nè dolcezza di figlio, nè la pieta
>   del vecchio padre, nè il debito amore,
>   lo qual dovea Penelope far lieta,
> vincer poter dentro da me l'ardore
>   ch'i'ebbi a divenir del mondo esperto,
>   e degli vizii umani e del valore . . .

> [When
> I departed from Circe, who detained
>   me more than a year there near Gaeta
>   before Aeneas named it thus,
> neither fondness for a son, nor duty
>   to my old father, nor the love owed Penelope
>   which should have made her glad,
> could overcome in me the burning desire
>   that I had to gain experience of the world,
>   and of the vices and the worth of men.] *

In the belief that Dante had transferred Sinon's sentiment to Ulysses, Edward Moore[2] noted these lines as the source for Ulysses' speech (*Aen.* 2. 137–38):

History of Greek Literature, trans. James Willis and Cornelius de Heer (New York: Crowell, 1966), pp. 42–43.

[2] Edward Moore, *Studies in Dante,* First Series: Scripture and Classical Authors in Dante (Oxford: Clarendon Press, 1896), p. 182.

*My translation.

nec mihi iam patriam antiquam spes ulla videndi,
nec dulcis natos exoptatumque parentem.

Pietro di Dante had cited a quite different line (*Aen.* 2. 666): "Ascanium patremque meum iuxtaque Creusam"— which makes somewhat more sense, in that we have son, father, and wife (and in that order, as Pietro pointed out).[3]

Pietro's citation gives us a hint of Dante's intention. While Ulysses was wandering around the Mediterranean, Aeneas and his men were also on a voyage, making their laborious way to Italy; and Dante is at some pains to establish Ulysses as an anti-Aeneas. Among Ulysses' crimes was "l'aguato del caval che fe' la porta/ onde uscì de' *Romani* il gentil *seme*" (cf. "Considerate la vostra *semenza*" at *Inf.* 26. 118); he refers to his being held by Circe near Gaeta "prima che sì Enea la nominasse"; and Ulysses' thoroughgoing rejection of *pieta(s)* makes him the opposite of *pius Aeneas*, who was introduced at the outset as "quel giusto figliuol d'Anchise, che venne da Troia" (*Inf.* 1. 73-74), and "di Silvio lo parente" (2. 13). And we may consider especially the way in which Ulysses inspires his men to make their final voyage (*Inf.* 26. 112-20):

> "O frati," dissi, "che per cento milia
>   perigli siete giunti all'occidente,
>   a questa tanto picciola vigilia
> de' nostri sensi ch'è del rimanente,
>   non vogliate negar l'esperienza,
>   diretro al sol, del mondo senza gente.
> Considerate la vostra semenza:

---

[3] Pietro's "curious comment" is mentioned by Moore, *ibid.*, p. 183, n. 1. Cf. also Venus's words to her son at 2. 596-98.

> fatti non foste a viver come bruti,
> ma per seguir virtute e conoscenza."

["O brothers," I said, "who through a hundred thousand
>> dangers have reached the West,
>> to this so brief vigil
> of our senses which is left,
>> do not deny the experience,
>> following the sun, of the world without men.
> Consider your origin:
>> you were not made to live like brutes,
>> but to follow virtue and knowledge."] *

For a comparable exhortation, the commentators naturally refer us to the speech in which Aeneas, after a storm has driven them off course to Africa, tries to encourage his men with hopes of better things to come (*Aen.* 1. 198–207):

> O socii (neque enim ignari sumus ante malorum),
> o passi graviora, dabit deus his quoque finem.
> vos et Scyllaeam rabiem penitusque sonantis
> accestis scopulos, vos et Cyclopia saxa
> experti: revocate animos maestumque timorem
> mittite; forsan et haec olim meminisse iuvabit.
> per varios casus, per tot discrimina rerum
> tendimus in Latium, sedes ubi fata quietas
> ostendunt; illic fas regna resurgere Troiae.
> durate, et vosmet rebus servate secundis.

> [Comrades, this is hardly our first adversity.
> You've suffered worse; this too the god will end.
> You sailed near Scylla's rage, the deep resounding
> crags, and know by trial the Cyclops' stones.
> Recall your courage, banish gloomy fear:

---

*My translation.

perhaps you'll enjoy remembering even this.
Through various calamities and hazards
we strive toward Latium, where the fates disclose
peaceful abodes: there Troy may rise again.
Endure and save yourselves for prosperous times.] *

But let us pursue our *Quellenforschung* a bit further. Aeneas's speech in turn had been modeled upon that in which Odysseus exhorted his men as they approached Scylla and Charybdis:

Reflect, my friends, that we are not untried in evil fortunes, nor in sadder plight are we than when within his spacious cave the brutal Cyclops held us prisoners; yet through my valor we escaped, and through my counsels and devices, and I think that you will live to bear this day's events in memory like those. . . .[4]

Thus, Ulysses' speech echoes, though indirectly and at a remove of some two thousand years, the words of his epic original. This would be worth remarking even if it were a mere accident of literary history, forming as it does a direct link between the greatest Greek poet, the greatest Latin poet, and the greatest poet of the Middle Ages. But it may be more than an accident.

Of course Dante and his contemporaries could not read Homer in the original. The tale of Troy had come down to Dante only through various Latin filters; so he could not compare texts in quite the same way we can. There was available to him, however, a compendium that remains handy even today—Macrobius's *Saturnalia*, the

---

[4]*Odyssey* 12. 208–12 (Bryant translation, slightly modified).

*My translation.

fifth book of which quotes numerous passages that Virgil allegedly borrowed from Homer.

With a generosity that has not characterized all critics before and after him, Eustathius (one of Macrobius's speakers) avers that Virgil improved upon his model at many points. As an example he quotes *Aeneid* 1. 198–203, along with *Odyssey* 12. 208–12, remarking that "Ulysses here reminded his comrades of a single calamity; Aeneas, on the other hand, bids his men hope for deliverance from their present ill fortune by a reference to the happy issue on two former occasions . . . . Moreover, in the lines that follow, your poet has gone on to give stronger grounds for comfort; for Aeneas encouraged his men not only by a reference to dangers escaped but by holding out hopes of happy days to come, promising them that their present toils would lead not only to a home and rest but to the restoration of their kingdom as well."[5] And although Aeneas at this point thinks merely of a revived Troy, the *regna* he promises will prove to be the *imperium Romanum* that plays such an important part in Dante's thought.[6]

Ulysses and his men are on their own, relying upon their innate qualities, in the pursuit of "virtute e conoscenza" on the sea. Aeneas, however, relying upon divine guidance ("deus dabit finem"), makes for a definite goal, his *patria* ("tendimus in Latium": cf. *Aen.* 4. 347: "hic

---

[5] *Saturnalia* 5. 11. 7–8, trans. Percival Vaughan Davies, in *Records of Civilization: Sources and Studies* (New York: Columbia University Press, 1969), 79: 324.

[6] See, especially, Charles Till Davis, *Dante and the Idea of Rome* (Oxford: Clarendon Press, 1957).

amor, haec patria est"). Moreover, Aeneas is just recovering from a shipwreck and about to begin his hesitating but fate-driven course to Italy, while Ulysses is starting a voyage that will end in shipwreck "com'altrui piacque." Ulysses' speech echoes that of Aeneas, but their differing situations and attitudes are a measure of the gulf between them, of the extent to which Ulysses appears as the antitype of Aeneas.

This contrast between Ulysses and Aeneas (which is ultimately a contrast between Greeks and Romans) is later reinforced implicitly by Dante's juxtaposition of materials. In *Purgatorio* 17, at the center of the poem, disordered love is shown to be the principle of sin; and then in the next Canto Dante witnesses the purgation of sloth on the fourth terrace. The examples of zeal are driven by "buon volere e giusto amor" (96), while in contrast, as examples of sloth, we have the Hebrews who did not make it to Canaan and the Trojans whom Aeneas had to leave behind in Sicily (133–38). Before he falls asleep, the last words Dante hears concern those who did not last to the end of the journey, those who had no heart for pushing on to their promised land. He then proceeds to dream about the siren who lured Ulysses off his course: Ulysses' divagation is measured against the steadfastness of Aeneas.

A similar pattern appears in the final cantica. Just before looking down at Ulysses' *varco folle*, Dante heard Peter's scathing denunciation of the Church, which ended (*Par.* 26. 58–63):

> Del sangue nostro Caorsini e Guaschi
>> s'apparecchian di bere; o buon principio,
>> a che vil fine convien che tu caschi!

> Ma l'alta provvidenza, che con Scipio
> > difese a Roma la gloria del mondo,
> > soccorrà tosto, sì com'io concipio.

> [Cahorsines and Gascons make ready
> > to drink our blood; o good beginning,
> > to what a base ending you must fall!
> But the lofty Providence that with Scipio
> > preserved for Rome the glory of the world,
> > will bring help soon, as I conceive.] *

Again, a reference to Roman glory precedes the reintroduction of Ulysses, and his mad course contrasts sharply with the providential course of Roman history.

Even more than the Hebrews, the Romans were—in Dante's eyes—a chosen people;[7] and this consideration should help us to appreciate the dramatic situation of *Inferno* 26. Between the false counsellor and the Christian poet (whose poetic testament is to be a form of counsel) stands Virgil, Dante's counsellor and the spur to Dante's journey. As Rome mediated between the pagan and the Christian worlds, so Virgil mediates between Ulysses and Dante, between the great figure of classical wisdom and the pilgrim pursuing a course which confounds that wisdom: "For the Jews require a sign, and the Greeks seek after wisdom: but we preach Christ crucified, unto the Jews a stumbling-block, and unto the Greeks foolishness; but unto them which are called, both Jews and Greeks,

---

[7]See W. H. V. Reade, "Dante's Vision of History," *Proceedings of the British Academy*, 25 (1939): 187–215.

*My translation.

Christ the power of God, and the wisdom of God. Because the foolishness of God is wiser than men; and the weakness of God is stronger than men."[8]

---

[8] I Corinthians 1: 22–25. On which text, see John Freccero, "The Sign of Satan," *Modern Language Notes*, 80 (1965): 11–26; and "Infernal Inversion and Christian Conversion (*Inferno* XXXIV)," *Italica*, 42 (1965): 35–41.

VIII

Ulysses
and
Dante

Dante's is not the only flight in the poem: Ulysses also describes a *volo*, this time a flight that failed (*Inf.* 26. 121–25):

> Li miei compagni fec' io sì acuti,
>> con questa orazion picciola, al cammino,
>> che appena poscia gli avrei ritenuti.
> E volta nostra poppa nel mattino,
>> de' remi facemmo ali al folle volo.[1]

[1] Line 125 is based on an ancient metaphor, *remigium alarum*, which Dante would have known especially from its use in the *Aeneid* (1. 301; 6. 19). It was adopted later to refer to the Christian's flight to God, e.g., by Augustine: "Neque vero cunctandum putes quomodo tibi volandum sit, quibus alarum remigiis. Dixit quidem David: quis dabit mihi pennas sicut columbae, et volabo et requiescam (Ps. LXVII, 14)," a passage quoted by Courcelle, "Quelques symboles funéraires du néo-platonisme latin," p. 68, n. 3. See also John Freccero, "Dante's Prologue Scene (I. The Region of Unlikeness; II. The Wings of Ulysses)," *Dante Studies*, 84 (1966): 1–25.

[With this brief speech I made
    my companions so eager for the journey
    that I could hardly then have held them back.
And with our stern turned toward the morning,
    of our oars we made wings for the mad flight.] *

At several other points, the *Inferno* establishes a parallel between Ulysses' voyage and Dante's present journey. We will recall that Ulysses urged his men to seek *esperienza*, and then we note that Virgil leads Dante through Hell "per dar lui esperienza piena" (*Inf.* 28. 48: "to give him full experience"). Ulysses' *cammino* must recall Dante's, just as the *alto passo* that Ulysses enters must bring to mind the *alto passo* at which Dante had hesitated (*Inf.* 2. 12). Moreover, in expressing his grave reservations, Dante had feared lest his journey be *folle* (*Inf.* 2. 35); and *folle* is the very word that both Ulysses and Dante apply to Ulysses' flight.

Then later, when Beatrice is passing judgment upon Dante, he confesses how he had gone astray (*Purg.* 31. 34–36):

Piangendo dissi: 'Le presenti cose
    col falso lor piacer volser miei passi,
    tosto che il vostro viso si nascose.'

[Weeping, I said: "Present things
    with their false pleasure turned my steps
    as soon as your face was hidden."] *

This *falso piacere* may well recall the siren's *piacere*, especially when Beatrice goes on to rebuke Dante in terms reminiscent of that dream (*Purg.* 31. 43–63):

*My translation.

64

Tuttavia, perchè mo vergogna porte
    del tuo errore, e perchè altra volta
    udendo le Sirene sie più forte,
pon giù il seme del piangere, ed ascolta;
    sì udirai come in contraria parte
    mover doveati mia carne sepolta.
Mai non t'appresentò natura o arte
    piacer, quanto le belle membra in ch'io
    rinchiusa fui, e sono in terra sparte:
e se il sommo piacer sì ti fallio
    per la mia morte, qual cosa mortale
    dovea poi trarre te nel suo disio?
Ben ti dovevi, per lo primo strale
    delle cose fallaci, levar suso
    diretro a me che non era più tale.
Non ti dovea gravar le penne in giuso,
    ad aspettar più colpi, o pargoletta,
    o altra vanità con sì breve uso.
Nuovo augelletto due o tre aspetta;
    ma dinanzi dagli occhi dei pennuti
    rete si spiega indarno o si saetta.

[Nevertheless, so that you may now feel shame
    for your wandering, and so that another time,
    hearing the Sirens, you may be stronger,
set aside the sowing of tears and listen;
    thus will you hear how my buried flesh
    should have moved you in the opposite direction.
Never did nature or art present to you
    delight equal to the fair members in which I
    was enclosed, and they are now scattered in earth;
and if the highest beauty thus failed you
    through my death, what mortal thing
    should have drawn you into desire for it?
Indeed you should, at the first shaft
    of deceptive things, have raised yourself up
    after me, who was no longer such.

> Your wings should not have been weighed down,
>   to await more hits, by a young woman
>   or other vanity of such brief use.
> A young bird waits for two or three;
>   but before the eyes of the full-fledged
>   the net is spread or the arrow shot in vain.] *

Instead of following the way set for him, Dante had flown off course, lured by the siren song. He had been something of a Ulysses, and we can further infer that Ulysses' metaphorical flight represents a spiritual course once pursued by Dante himself until it ended in disaster.

This much is suggested by Dante's text; but it may well be objected, why speak of a "spiritual course"? Did not Ulysses' siren represent the temptations of the flesh?[2] And what is so spiritual about Dante's siren-like *pargoletta*? Is Dante not simply confessing that he had indeed been attracted by the *donna pietosa* after Beatrice's death?[3] Perhaps. But Dante's confrontation with Beatrice is the central event of the poem and the climax of the most important relationship of his life;[4] and unless we wish to assume that Beatrice is displaying, after all those years, an inordinate feminine pique, we had best assume

[2] This is assumed even by Joseph Mazzeo, whose argument otherwise anticipates mine in some respects; see his "Appendix: The 'Sirens' of *Purgatorio* XXXI, 45," *Medieval Cultural Tradition in Dante's "Comedy"* (Ithaca: Cornell University Press, 1960), pp. 205–12.

[3] For a brief discussion of the evidence on this whole question, see *La Divina Commedia di Dante Alighieri*, ed. C. H. Grandgent, rev. ed. (Boston: Heath, 1933), pp. 612–14.

[4] See Charles Singleton, *Dante Studies 1: Commedia: Elements*, pp. 45–60.

*My translation.

that Dante's charmer was more than just a Florentine *augelletta*.[5] To grasp her significance, and the significance of Dante's relation to Ulysses, we shall have to move for a moment outside the poem itself; for Beatrice's accusation must be viewed within the context of Dante's whole literary and spiritual career, and that career must be viewed within a far more ancient context.

We observed earlier that in late antiquity Ulysses had become a figure of *sapientia* and his journey an allegory for the journey of the soul. So rich was his story in metaphorical implications that many authors had this paradigm in mind even when they did not mention Ulysses explicitly, as in Plotinus's description of the contemplative (*Enneads* 5. 9. 1). Augustine also used Ulysses' voyage as a paradigm for the *vita philosophica*. He develops the metaphor brilliantly in the preface to his *De Beata Vita*, written when he was much under the influence of the Neoplatonists;[6] and if this were his last word on the subject of philosophy, we might well construe Ulysses' voyage as a noble Augustinian endeavor. But later Augustine took quite a different view of the philosophic texts he had once embraced; and the central chapters of the *Confessions* are an impassioned polemic against the Platonists. Disillusioned at length with his former course, Augustine embarks upon another journey: "Et inde monitus redire ad memet ipsum intravi in intima mea duce te et potui, quoniam factus es adiutor meus" (7. 10. 16: "And admon-

---

[5] Cf. also Beatrice's later reference to "quella scuola ch' hai seguitata" (*Purg.* 33. 85–86), and the ensuing conversation between her and Dante.

[6] On Augustine's Neoplatonism, see Pierre Courcelle, *Recherches sur les Confessions de Saint Augustin* (Paris: Boccard, 1950). For a discussion of the preface to *De Beata Vita*, see Freccero, "Dante's Prologue Scene."

ished by this to return to my own self, I entered into the innermost part of me with your guidance, and I was able to since you became my helper").

The philosophic voyage is not the way after all; and Augustine could well agree with the warning issued by his contemporary, Paulinus of Nola:

Esto Peripateticus Deo, Pythagoreus mundo; verae in Christo sapientiae praedicator, et tandem tacitus vanitati, perniciosam istam inanium dulcedinem litterarum, quasi illos patriae oblitteratores de baccarum suavitate Lotophagos, et Sirenarum carmina, blandimentorum nocentium cantus evita. . . . [Sirenas] oportet ultra Ulyxis astutiam cauti non auribus tantum, sed et oculis obseratis et animo navigio praetervolante fugiamus, ne sollicitati delectatione letifera in criminum saxa rapiamur et scopulo mortis adfixi naufragium salutis obeamus.[7]

[Be a Peripatetic for God and a Pythagorean as regards the world. Preach the true wisdom that lies in Christ, and be finally silent towards what is vain. Avoid this destructive sweetness of empty literature as you would the Lotus-eaters, who made men forget their fatherland by the sweetness of their berries, or as you would the Sirens' songs, those melodies of baneful seduction. . . . We must avoid them by being cleverer than Ulysses, blocking not only our ears but also our eyes and our mind, as it sails like a ship swiftly by, so that we may not be seduced by the delight that brings death and drawn on to the rocks of sin, be caught on the crags of death and suffer the shipwreck of our salvation.[8]]

[7]Quoted by Courcelle, *REA*, (1944), p. 89, n. 3. On the same page Courcelle notes Cicero's assertion that the sirens really offered knowledge (*De finibus* 5. 18. 49); and Mazzeo, *Medieval Cultural Traditions*, makes good use of this passage in Cicero.

[8]*Letters of Paulinus of Nola*, trans. and annotated by P. C. Walsh, Ancient Christian Writers, no. 35 (Westminster, Maryland: Newman Press, 1966), 1: 158–59 (Letter 16.7).

As Courcelle observes: "C'est la lecture des philosophes qui est interdite; l'héroïsation par la culture est, au gré de Paulin, un erreur funeste."

Therefore there are excellent grounds for seeing Ulysses' voyage as a philosophic flight, and the sirens as not carnal but intellectual temptations. Now Dante's two major changes in the Ulysses story were (1) having his homeward journey broken off by a quest for knowledge; and (2) having him diverted by the sirens. The legendary and allegorical Ulysses did no such things. On this all authorities were agreed. But if our inference that Ulysses' voyage represents an earlier enterprise of Dante's is correct, then Dante's career should evidence a similar divagation. This is exactly the case.

If we are prepared to view the sirens as intellectual temptations, we may also be prepared to take Dante at his word when he claims that the *donna pietosa* was really Lady Philosophy. To Grandgent, Dante's attempt to convince us of this in the *Convivio* was a glaring instance of bad faith on his part; and he remarks that "it is noteworthy that this treatise was never finished. Dante's conscience, apparently, was ill at ease; and here, in the *Commedia*, he at last tells the whole truth, admitting that his love for the *pargoletta* was not merely an innocent devotion to that 'figlia d'Iddio, regina di tutto, nobilissima e bellissima Filosofia' (*Conv.* 2. 13. 71–72), but also, and originally, a sentiment deserving reprobation."[9] There certainly was such a real lady; for she appeared in the *Vita Nuova*. But Dante never says that the lady represented *only* Lady Philosophy, that he wished to allegorize her

[9] Grandgent, *La Divina Commedia*, p. 613.

away. His lengthy explanation of the literal level of his canzone (*Voi che intendendo*) should suggest that there was something real there to talk about. Indeed, James E. Shaw showed that there is no real contradiction between the lady's being real and her being a symbol of philosophy according to the author's "sentenza vera." The one does not cancel the other.[10]

Therefore, when a real Beatrice accuses Dante of having been lured off course by a real lady, we need not call this a renunciation of his former allegory or rush to judgment upon Dante himself. Instead, we should read her speech as a denunciation of Dante's own former pursuit of "virtute e conoscenza" in his philosophical-ethical treatise, the *Convivio*.

Ulrich Leo documented in great detail the fundamental differences between the *Convivio* on the one hand and the *Vita Nuova* and *Commedia* on the other. In the *Convivio*, the author's guides are reason and faith, while in the works concerned with Beatrice they are seeing and vision; and "it is evident that, once the poet's spirit found itself filled with this greatest of all his religious symbols—the experience of his eyes confronted with the reality of supernatural light, a symbol which, besides being religious more than philosophical, is *poetic and not prosaic*—he had to renounce his philosophical and ethical prose writing, *per correr migliori acque* of religious poetry."[11]

---

[10]See James E. Shaw, *The Lady "Philosophy" in the "Convivio"* (Cambridge, Mass.: Dante Society, 1938).

[11]Ulrich Leo, "The Unfinished *Convivio* and Dante's Rereading of the *Aeneid*," *Sehen und Wirklichkeit bei Dante* (Frankfort: Klostermann, 1957), p. 90.

This important distinction still does not explain why Dante "had to" abandon the *Convivio*. The *Commedia* represents a return to the mode of direct vision, which Dante had originally followed before going off on an abortive philosophical flight. But this venture into philosophy was not just another way of writing which Dante could assume or drop as his muse required. In Beatrice's terms, it was a falling away that had brought Dante nearly to damnation (*Purg.* 30. 121–38):

Alcun tempo il sostenni col mio volto;
    mostrando gli occhi giovinetti a lui,
    meco il menava in dritta parte volto.
Sì tosto come in sulla soglia fui
    di mia seconda etade, e mutai vita,
    questi si tolse a me, e diessi altrui.
Quando di carne a spirto era salita,
    e bellezza e virtù cresciuta m'era,
    fu'io a lui men cara e men gradita;
e volse i passi suoi per via non vera,
    imagini di ben seguendo false,
    che nulla promission rendono intera.
Nè impetrare ispirazion mi valse
    con le quali ed in sogno ed altrimenti
    lo rivocai; sì poco a lui ne calse.
Tanto giù cadde, che tutti argomenti
    alla salute sua eran già corti,
    fuor che mostrargli le perdute genti.

[For a time I sustained him with my countenance;
    showing my youthful eyes to him
    I led him with me, turned in the right direction.
As soon as I was on the threshold
    of my second age, and I changed life,
    he took himself from me and gave himself to another.

When I had risen from flesh to spirit,
  and beauty and virtue had increased in me,
  I was to him less dear and less pleasing;
and he turned his steps on a way not true,
  following false images of good,
  which fulfill no promise.
And it did not avail me to obtain inspirations,
  with which in dream and otherwise
  I called him back; so little did he heed them.
He fell so low, that all means
  for his salvation were now insufficient,
  except to show him the lost people.] *

Or in Paulinus's terms, Dante had been heading for a *naufragium salutis*; and we need hardly wonder at the harshness of Beatrice's indictment.

Ulysses' voyage is an image of the misguided philosophical Odyssey; and Dante's dream in *Purgatorio* 19 dramatizes how he saw the light, with the aid of Virgil and Beatrice. The *Convivio* is unfinished because it represented a *via non vera* that led toward spiritual shipwreck: Philosophy cannot do what Boethius's lady had claimed,[12] and Dante must make a different journey—the Augustinian journey into the self.

In this perspective, we can appreciate the apparently gratuitous allusion to Ulysses at the end of *Purgatorio* 1. Dante had already represented himself as a shipwreck in the metaphorical equivalent of the waters in which Ulysses

[12] See Boethius, *De Consolatione Philosophiae* 4. 1: ". . . viam tibi quae te domum revehat ostendam. Pennas etiam tuae menti quibus se in altum tollere possit adfigam, ut perturbatione depulsa sospes in patriam meo ductu, mea semita, meis etiam vehiculis revertaris."

*My translation.

drowned;[13] and when Dante and Virgil walk along the shore "com'uom che torna alla perduta strada" (*Purg.* 1. 119: "like one returning to the road he has lost"), it marks his return to the way Beatrice had set for him in the first place, the *via salutis* that he had for a while abandoned. Ulysses comes to ruin where he does not because he violated a divine prohibition in approaching the mountain, but because Dante wants him there to emphasize the contrast between his own present upward course and his own previous *folle volo*.[14]

[13]See Singleton, *Dante Studies 1: Commedia: Elements*, pp. 5–12; and Freccero, *Harvard Theological Review*, 1959, pp. 247 ff.

[14]Thus both Nardi and Montano are partially right. The Dante of the *Convivio* does indeed find expression in Ulysses: our author writes whereof he knows. And this earlier Dante is judged by his post-conversion successor, who might well agree with much of the critique that Montano levels against that same Ulysses.

IX

Aeneas
and
Dante

In adapting the Ulysses story to depict his own spiritual autobiography, Dante plays Ulysses off against Aeneas. It might be well then, in conclusion, to inquire whether Aeneas also has a peculiar relevance to Dante's *itinerarium mentis.*

At first sight there appears to be more difference than similarity between the pagan hero and the Christian pilgrim. Asking the Sibyl for her help, Aeneas observes that others have descended to Avernus before him, and claims an equal right (*Aen.* 6. 119–23):

> si potuit manis accersere coniugis Orpheus
> Threicia fretus cithara fidibusque canoris,
> si fratrem Pollux alterna morte redemit
> itque reditque viam totiens. quid Thesea, magnum
> quid memorem Alciden? et mi genus ab Iove summo.

> [If Orpheus, relying on his Thracian lyre,
> was able to summon forth his wife's shade;

if Pollux redeemed his brother, dying by turns,
going back and forth so often—why mention Theseus,
or mighty Hercules?—I too descend from Jove supreme.] *

Dante also refers to his predecessors, but to make just the
opposite point—he is not Prince Aeneas, nor was meant to
be (*Inf.* 2. 13–15, 28–33):

Tu dici che di Silvio lo parente
    corruttibile ancora, ad immortale
    secolo andò, e fu sensibilmente.
. . . .
Andovvi poi lo Vas d'elezione
    per recarne conforto a quella fede
    che è principio alla via di salvazione.
Ma io perchè venirvi? o chi'l concede?
    Io non Enea, io non Paolo sono:
    me degno a ciò nè io nè altri 'l crede.

[You say that the father of Silvius
    still subject to corruption, went bodily
    to the eternal world.
. . . .
Later the Chosen Vessel went there
    to bring back comfort to that faith
    which is the beginning of the way to salvation.
But I, why should I go there? Who grants it?
    I am not Aeneas, I am not Paul:
    neither I nor any one thinks me worthy of that.] *

On the face of it, Dante's disclaimer seems obvious
enough: confronted with the prospect of going to the
other world while still in this life, he denies any similarity
between himself and two heroes who had supposedly done
just that. More specifically, Aeneas's *descensus ad inferos*

*My translation.

would correspond to the first stage of the journey ahead of Dante, whereas Paul had told of a visit to Dante's celestial goal: "I knew a man in Christ above fourteen years ago, (whether in the body, I cannot tell; or whether out of the body, I cannot tell: God knoweth;) such an one caught up to the third heaven. And I knew such a man . . . how that he was caught up into paradise, and heard unspeakable words, which it is not lawful for a man to utter" (II Corinthians 12: 2–4).

Paul's brief account (of what was generally taken to be his own experience) is certainly more suggestive than specific; but in Augustine and Aquinas's interpretations the *raptus Pauli* became the great exemplar of *visio intellectualis,* that is, the direct, unmediated, and indescribable knowledge of God which Dante himself attains at the end of his journey.[1]

As for Aeneas, Virgil's account of his descent was of course the major literary precedent for a physical journey to the other world by a man "in the body." But as we have seen, to a medieval reader the *Aeneid,* too, was more than just a history of physical events; and Bernard Silvestris's interpretation of Aeneas's *iter* may be directly relevant to the specific configuration of Dante's spiritual itinerary.

Glossing Aeneas's vision of Anchises near the end of book 5, Bernard says (27.25–28.1):

Monetur imagine patris ad inferos descendere visurus patrem ibi i. e. cogitatione quadam imaginaria quam de creatore habet. Non enim perfectam potest habere, cum deus incircumscriptus sit cogitatione. In qua ille monetur, ut ad mundana per cognitionem descendat,

---

[1] See Francis X. Newman, "St. Augustine's Three Visions and the Structure of the *Commedia,*" *Modern Language Notes*, 82 (1967): 56–78.

ibique videbit patrem quia quamvis in creaturis non sit, cognitione tamen creaturarum cognoscitur. Ideoque iubetur apud inferos quaerere patrem licet celsa inhabitat.

[He is advised by an image of his father to descend to the infernal regions to see his father there; that is, by some imaginary thought which he has of the creator, for it cannot be perfect, since God is not circumscribed by thought. In it he is advised to descend for knowledge to worldly things, and there he will see his father; for although he is not in creatures, nevertheless he is known through a knowledge of creatures. And so he is ordered to seek his father among the infernal regions, although he dwells on high.] *

Then in the introduction to his word-by-word commentary on book 6, Bernard discusses the descent of the soul in some detail. Initially, his explanations derive quite directly from Macrobius, who had observed that a *descensus ad inferos* could signify the soul's descent into the body:

antequam studium philosophiae circa naturae inquisitionem ad tantum vigoris adolesceret, qui per diversas gentes auctores constituendis sacris caerimoniarum fuerunt, aliud esse inferos negaverunt quam ipsa corpora, quibus inclusae animae carcerem foedum tenebris, horridum sordibus et cruore patiuntur.[2]

[Before the zeal of philosophers for the study of natural science grew to such vigorous proportions, those who were responsible for establishing religious rites among different races insisted that the lower regions were nothing more than the mortal bodies themselves,

---

[2]*Commentarii in Somnium Scipionis*, ed. Iacobus Willis (Teubner: Leipzig, 1963), I. 10. 9 (p. 43). The English version following is from *Commentary on the Dream of Scipio*, trans. William Harris Stahl (New York: Columbia University Press, 1952), p. 128.

*My translation.

shut up in which souls suffered a horrible punishment in vile darkness and blood.]

Modifying Macrobius somewhat, Bernard begins as follows (28.15-18):

Antequam philosophia ad id vigoris adolesceret, theologiae professores aliud esse inferos quam corpora humana negaverunt, inferos autem corpora dixerunt eo quod in rebus nichil aliud inferius invenerunt.

[Before philosophy grew to its present vigorous proportions, the teachers of theology insisted that the lower regions were nothing more than human bodies, since among things they found nothing lower.] *

Macrobius goes on in his next chapter to note that the Platonists gave *inferi* a more extensive meaning (or rather, several more extensive meanings, since three groups are discussed). Some called our perishable sublunary realm the infernal regions of the dead (9.6); and Bernard concludes with a reference to this "caducam et inferiorem regionem" (29.27).

However, the final and most interesting part of Bernard's introduction to book 6 seems to be his own invention.[3] There are, he explains, four kinds of *descensus ad inferos*. The first is every man's Fall (30.3-7):

[3]Cf. Stanislaus Skimina, "De Bernardo Silvestri Vergilii Interprete," seorsum impressum ex *Commentationibus Vergilianis* (Cracow, 1930), 237-38: "Restat ut dicamus Bernardum, etiamsi aliorum libros exscriberet, quos quidem maxima libertate immutaret, multa addidisse quae eum ingeniosum atque inventionis vi praeditum fuisse ostendant." Skimina does observe, however, "Quorum nonnulla tam nova sunt adeoque praeter omnem opinionem accidunt, ut in incerto simus, utrum seriarum an iocosarum interpretationum loco numeranda sint."

*My translation.

Naturalis est nativitas hominis: ea enim naturaliter incipit anima esse in hac caduca regione atque ita inferis descendere atque ita a divinitate sua recedere et paulatim in vitium declinare et carnis voluptatibus assentire: sed iste omnium communis est.

[The natural descent is the birth of man; for by it the soul naturally begins to be in this perishable region and thus descend to the infernal world, departing thus from its divinity and gradually turning aside to vice and assenting to the pleasures of the flesh. But that is the common lot of all men.] *

Most important in this context is the second sort of descent, made by Orpheus and Hercules (30.7–12):

Est autem alius virtutis qui fit dum sapiens aliquis ad mundana per considerationem descendit, non ut in eis intentionem ponat sed ut eorum cognita fragilitate eis abiectis ad invisibilia penitus se convertat et creaturarum cognitione creatorem evidentius agnoscat.

[There is, however, another descent, of virtue, which takes place when some wise man descends to worldly things for contemplation, not to concentrate on them, but so that having perceived their fragility he may cast them aside and turn himself completely to invisible things and through a knowledge of creatures may perceive the creator more clearly.] *

Bernard later glosses *iter* as *ascensiones per creaturarum agnitiones*, explaining that the first step is from inanimate to insensible animate things, thence to irrational animals, rational animals ("i. e. ad homines," Bernard adds, with the optimism of an earlier age), the celestial orders, and finally to God: "Itaque per ordinem creaturarum itum est

*My translation.

ad creatorem" (52.22: "And so through a succession of creatures one goes to the creator").[4]

Charles Singleton has glossed the three lights in the *Commedia* with the following statement by Aquinas: "There is a kind of vision for which the natural light of intellect suffices, such as the contemplation of invisible things according to the principles of reason; and the philosophers placed the highest happiness of man in this contemplation; there is yet another kind of contemplation to which man is raised by the light of faith . . . and there is that contemplation of the blessed in Heaven [*in patria*] to which the intellect is uplifted by the light of Glory"—which sometimes happens, as in Paul's case, to a man still in this life.[5] These three lights do not correspond to the tripartite division of the *Commedia*, for it is Beatrice who gives Dante wings for flight (*Par.* 10. 53–54), and his whole flight to God is a transhumanizing, a going beyond the human (*Par.* 1. 70: "trasumanar"), while his movement under Virgil's guidance was by the natural light of intellect.[6] *Inferno* and *Purgatorio* mark a first ontological stage, *Paradiso* a second.

---

[4] Although Bernard's is not a Christianizing interpretation of the *Aeneid*, and there are obviously some elements in his commentary which would be difficult to square with Christian doctrine, he had good patristic sanction for the idea that pagans could know God through his creation. For example, in discussing the similarity between Platonism and Christianity, Augustine three times (*De civitate Dei* 8.6, 10, 12) cites Romans I:19–20: "Quia quod notum est Dei, manifestum est in illis; Deus enim illis manifestavit. Invisibilia enim ipsius, a creatura mundi, per ea quae facta sunt, intellecta, conspiciuntur; sempiterna quoque eius virtus, et divinitas."

[5] Singleton, *Dante Studies 2: Journey to Beatrice*, p. 15.

[6] See Singleton, *Journey*, esp. pp. 26–31. A basically bipartite division of the poem is also suggested by Dante's use of classical mythology. See C. A.

In discussing man's threefold knowledge of divine things, Aquinas said: "prima est secundum quod homo naturali lumine rationis per creaturas in Dei cognitionem ascendit" (the first is when man, by the natural light of reason, rises through creatures to the knowledge of God)[7]—exactly the mediated, partial vision to which Bernard refers, vision that is not yet *facie ad faciem.* Thus, if Aquinas's whole formulation is a fair gloss upon the *Commedia,* Bernard's allegorized *Aeneid* assumes a striking resemblance to the Virgilian first stage of Dante's journey.

Virgil can lead Dante only so far: then Beatrice must take over. At this crucial point in the poem, as if to underline the parallelism between his own *iter* and that of Aeneas, Dante quotes from the climactic episode of *Aeneid* 6 (*Purg.* 30. 19–21):

> Tutti dicean: *Benedictus qui venis,*
> e fior gittando di sopra e dintorno,
> *manibus o date lilia plenis.*

> [All were saying: *Benedictus qui venis,*
> and, throwing flowers above and around,
> *manibus o date lilia plenis.*][8] *

Robson, "Dante's Use in the *Divina Commedia* of the Medieval Allegories on Ovid," in *Centenary Essays on Dante,* by members of the Oxford Dante Society (Oxford: Clarendon Press, 1965), pp. 1–38.

[7]Quoted by Singleton, *Journey,* 36, 23. The passage is also cited by Silverstein, "Dante and Vergil the Mystic," p. 78.

[8]Dante is adapting *Aen.* 6. 883: *manibus date lilia plenis* (give lilies with full hands).

*My translation.

Christian and pagan: the one *iter* supersedes the other, but in so doing arises from and incorporates its predecessor.[9]

Before flying aloft to see God face to face, Dante undergoes a *descensus*, a *conversio* and an *ascensio*: he travels the same spiritual path along which the Sibyl had led Aeneas. Both journeys have the same pattern and the same basic epistemology. So despite his initial protestation, Dante becomes both an Enea and a Paolo, in quest of the heavenly *patria*, "quella Roma onde Cristo è romano" (*Purg.* 32. 102: "that Rome in which Christ is a Roman"). And it should be little cause for wonder if Bernard's mystic Virgil acts as his first guide, along that "cammino alto e silvestro" (*Inf.* 2. 142).

[9]Cf. Davis, *Dante and the Idea of Rome*, p. 33: "Christ came, and Peter established the see of Rome, not to interrupt the tradition, but to fulfill it." Davis cites (p. 138) *Purg.* 30. 19-21 to illustrate Virgil's "dual role" as intermediary between the two Romes; but the historicity and historical importance of Virgil and Aeneas do not preclude allegorical significances, since in Dante's view a figure could be both historical and allegorical. The historical process is development, metamorphosis; and the same holds for a man's psychological progress. See *Purg.* 10. 124-26; *Par.* 1. 67-72; and Singleton, *Journey*, p. 28-29.

Library of Congress Cataloging in Publication Data

Thompson, David, 1938-
  Dante's epic journeys.

  Includes bibliographical references.
  1. Dante Alighieri, 1265–1321—Allegory and
symbolism. 2. Vergilius Maro, Publius. Aeneis.
3. Homerus. Odyssea. I. Title.
PQ4406.T5   851'.1   73-8112
ISBN 0-8018-1518-5

THE JOHNS HOPKINS UNIVERSITY PRESS

This book was composed in Aldine Roman text and Bookman Italic
display type by Jones Composition Company, Inc., from a design by
Beverly Baum. It was printed on 70-lb. Regency Laid stock and
bound in Holliston Roxite cloth by Universal Lithographers, Inc.